Tattletale Tilly

Joanna Weaver
Illustrated by Tony Kenyon

To my sweet nephew and niece,
Ross and Taylor Brown:
You love each other so well!

Faith Kids® is an imprint of Cook Communications Ministries,
Colorado Springs, Colorado 80918
Cook Communications, Paris, Ontario
Kingsway Communications, Eastbourne, England

TATTLETALE TILLY
© 2001 by Joanna Weaver for text and Tony Kenyon for illustrations

Editor: Kathy Davis
Graphic Design: Granite Design
First printing, 2001
Printed in Singapore
04 03 02 01 05   5 4 3 2 1

Library of Congress Cataloging-in-Publication Data

This book belongs to:

Jacob & Jonah

Love,
Joanna
Weaver

"You shall not go about as a talebearer
among your people."
Leviticus 19:16 (NKJV)

Tattletale Tilly, the youngest O'Toole,
 made sure those around her kept every rule.

From her big sister Milly to her big brother Tom,
Tilly kept them in line with her threats to tell Mom.

She monitored snacks, made sure homework was done.
Tilly made it hard to have any fun.

Even her friends
    and her classmates at school
knew Tilly would tell
    if they broke any rule.

"No cutting in line."
  "No cheating on tests."
"No blowing bubbles."
  "No gum under desks."
"Don't peek at playtime."
  "Don't pick up that snail!"
"The rules are the rules,"
  said the school tattletale.

At home Tilly tattled as much—even more!
     She'd rattle off lists of transgressions galore.
"MOM-mee!" she'd holler, her voice shrill with a plea.
     "You'd better come quickly and see what I see!"
"Milly did this . . ." and "Tommy did that . . ."
     "Why, I even saw what he did to the cat!"

ee!

All through the winter and into the spring
Tilly tattled and told about each little thing.

"Unh-unh-uh!" she would lecture, wagging her finger,
till her brother and sister just wanted to wring her.

"MOM-mee, Milly's sneezing."
"MOM-mee, Tommy's breathing!"

"Now, Tilly," said her mother, "I told you to drop it."
"I can't," whined poor Tilly. "They just have to stop it!"

Soon Tattletale Tilly had the family divided,
until they sat down and finally decided.

"Enough is enough!" their dad firmly said.
"But, but, but . . ." Tilly stuttered, her face turning red.

"You tell on your family.
	You tell on your friends.
I'm telling you, Tilly,
	this tattling must end."

Tilly paused for a moment, then admitted, "It's true . . .
I'm terrible 'bout tattling—it's so easy to do."
Her father said, "Tilly, talebearing's a sin.
Your problem, dear daughter, comes from within."

So Tattletale Tilly, the youngest O'Toole,
   asked God to forgive her and make her heart new.

20

"I'm thankful, dear Jesus, You don't tattle on me.
Give me Your eyes, Lord, and help me to see
the good things in people and not just the bad.
I want to be like You and make Your heart glad."

Well, of course Jesus helped her.
Soon Tilly O'Toole
stopped prattling and tattling
about every rule.

It took self-control,
    but once Tilly stopped squealing,
she found that her family
    was truly appealing!

They played happily all week, till one day at two o'clock,
when Tattletale Tilly was heard 'round the block.
"MOM-mee!" she yelled, her voice shrill with a plea.
"You'd better come quickly and see what I see!"

"Oh, no," sighed her mom,
    "I thought tattling had ended."
But then on the front porch,
    she saw something splendid.

27

There sat her children
    with three giant grins,
sucking on Popsicles
    with purple-streaked chins.
"MOM-mee!" laughed Tilly,
    her face filled with glee.
"Milly and Tom split their
    Popsicles with me."

So Tattletale Tilly, the youngest O'Toole,
  learned not to tattle at home or at school.
Instead of finding fault, little Tilly found it true:
  When you look for the best, the best comes to you!

"Love isn't selfish or quick tempered.
It doesn't keep a record of wrongs that others do."
1 Corinthians 13:5 (CEV)

Tattletale Tilly

Ages: 4-7

Life Issue: My child is learning to control his or her tongue.

Spiritual Building Block: Self-control

Learning Styles

Sight: After reading the story, look again at the pictures in the book. Ask your child to point to Tilly in each picture that shows her tattling. Then look at the children in those pictures. Ask: How do you think the children feel when Tilly tattles on them for things that aren't really wrong? What does Tilly need to do differently? (She needs to control her tongue, choosing words that help and don't hurt.)

Sound: Work with your child to repeat the Bible verse from the end of the story until you both have it memorized. Help your child list the kinds of wrongs we should ignore (mainly things that just bother us, or minor infractions of rules). Talk about the difference between tattling about small issues and alerting an adult to a truly dangerous activity or problem.

Touch: Together, you and your child can create a concrete reminder of the lesson presented in this story. Have your child draw a funny, happy face on a paper plate, cutting out a section 2" x 1" in the center of the mouth. Write the verse, "Love . . . doesn't keep a record of wrongs that others do," (1 Cor. 13:5) on a strip of red construction paper. Roll it up and tape the top end to the plate's back, inside the mouth slot. The message should unroll like an extra-long tongue!